Surviving

Please visit our website at: www.garethstevens.com
For a free color catalog describing Gareth Stevens'
list of high-quality books and multimedia programs,
call 1-800-542-2595 (USA) or 1-800-461-9120 (Canada).
Gareth Stevens Publishing's Fax: (414) 332-3567.

Library of Congress Cataloging-in-Publication Data available upon request from publisher. Fax (414) 336-0157 for the attention of the Publishing Records Department.

ISBN 0-8368-2933-6

This North American edition first published in 2001 by
Gareth Stevens Publishing
330 West Olive Street, Suite 100
Milwaukee, WI 53212 USA

© QA International, 2001

Created and produced as *So Many Ways to Live in Difficult Conditions* by

QA INTERNATIONAL
329 rue de la Commune Ouest, 3ᵉ étage
Montréal, Québec
Canada H2Y 2E1
Tel.: (514) 499-3000 Fax: (514) 499-3010
www.qa-international.com

Printed in Canada

1 2 3 4 5 6 7 8 9 05 04 03 02 01

Gareth Stevens Publishing
A WORLD ALMANAC EDUCATION GROUP COMPANY

Adapting to any conditions

Heat, water, light, and oxygen are just some of the elements necessary for life. However, certain areas of the world lack some of the things living beings need. Burning deserts, freezing ice floes, and the darkest depths of the oceans are some of the places where it is difficult for animals to exist. But some brave creatures go to great lengths to adapt to these hostile locations.

Life in slow motion

The sloth lives in the hot, humid South American tropical forests. To survive, this mammal conserves its energy. It sleeps over 15 hours a day and doesn't move around much. The fur of the sloth looks like the surrounding forest and sheds rainwater straight to the ground.

brown-throated three-toed sloth

Underwater vents

The floor of the Pacific contains vents that spew water from the depths of our planet. This liquid, which contains many chemicals, can be as hot as 750 degrees Fahrenheit (400° Celsius)! Giant worms, hidden inside stiff tubes, live near the vents and feed on the energy-rich compounds produced by bacteria.

hydrothermal vent tube worm

Adapting to changes

peppered moth

There are two types of peppered moths — black and white. More white moths existed before the coal industry developed, but then things changed. Black moths could hide from their predators on soot-covered tree trunks. White moths adapted to this pollution by giving birth to black offspring.

3

Freed by water

The lungfish can survive even if the stream in which it lives dries up! Thanks to its lungs, it can breathe in the open air, but it does something even more amazing. It wraps itself in a cocoon of hardened mucus that protects it until a rainfall dissolves its prison and returns the fish to its stream.

lungfish

Are you curious?

Green algae coat the damp hair of the sloth. These algae give the sloth's fur a green tinge that blends in with the forest vegetation and helps camouflage the mammal.

Desert animals

With temperatures that often reach 100 degrees Fahrenheit (38° C) and dry winds that whip up a sea of sand, the world's deserts are among the most hostile environments on Earth. They are home to about 5,000 species of animals that must adapt to survive. To avoid the sun, some take refuge underground in layers of sand; others hide in the shadows of shrubs or rocks or in humid burrows. Some animals find more extreme means of survival.

Ship of the desert

The dromedary, or one-humped camel, lives up to its nickname "ship of the desert." This mammal is equipped for long treks through the desert. It has hairy ears; eyes with long, thick lashes; and nostrils that can close to protect it from sandstorms. A reserve of fat on its back provides the camel with energy when food and water are scarce.

4

dromedary

Are you curious?

A great water saver, the dromedary sweats very little. It produces dry excrement and just a small amount of urine. After going without water for a long period of time, the dromedary can drink up to 26.5 gallons (100 liters), which it stores in its body for hard times ahead.

Cooling ears

The smallest fox of all escapes the desert heat by using its long, broad ears as an air conditioning system. The ears help get rid of heat from its body. But this little animal has more than one trick up its sleeve. To escape the intense daytime heat, it spends most of its time underground in the coolness of its den!

fennec

Dancing on the sand

Namib Desert sand dune lizard

Unlike mammals and birds, reptiles cannot regulate their body temperature. To keep its body from getting too hot, the Namib Desert sand dune lizard dances! It keeps two feet in the air at all times to avoid absorbing the heat of the desert sand.

Saving water

The heat of the Australian desert is often made worse by a lack of rain. Water-holding frogs bury themselves about 3 feet (1 meter) under the sand to await the next rainfall. Their two-layered skin forms a pocket that fills with water. Protected from dehydration, some of these frogs can lie dormant for up to 5 years!

water-holding frog

Finding water

Desert animals rarely find a reliable source of water. Tropical rain forests in North America receive up to 10 feet (3 m) of water each year. Deserts receive barely 0.8 inch (2 centimeters). Some deserts remain completely dry for years on end! Desert animals must do all they can to conserve water. Often, they must make do with only the liquid in the food they eat.

Winged sponges

Spotted sandgrouses constantly move around in search of water. When they find it, the male crouches in the water, shakes his body to absorb water, and stores it in special feathers on his belly. When the feathers are soaked with the precious liquid, the sandgrouse returns to his nest to water his offspring.

spotted sandgrouse

Desert humidifiers

The thick shell of the desert darkling beetle protects its body from the burning rays of the Sun. But that's not all! Beneath its hindquarters is a chamber that cools and humidifies air before it enters the insect's body. This "humidifier" keeps the beetle from becoming dehydrated.

desert darkling beetle

The rat that never drinks

The kangaroo rats of the North American deserts are the champions of saving water! Their food — dry seeds, leaves, and stems — provides the rodents with the water they need. To retain as much water as possible, they do not sweat and produce very little urine.

desert kangaroo rat

Turning fat into water

The spiny-tailed lizard can live through the droughts of the North African deserts. Beneath the skin on its back is fat that can turn into a water supply. A chemical transforms this fat during dry periods. The spiny-tailed lizard never drinks and can go without food for almost a year!

African spiny-tailed lizard

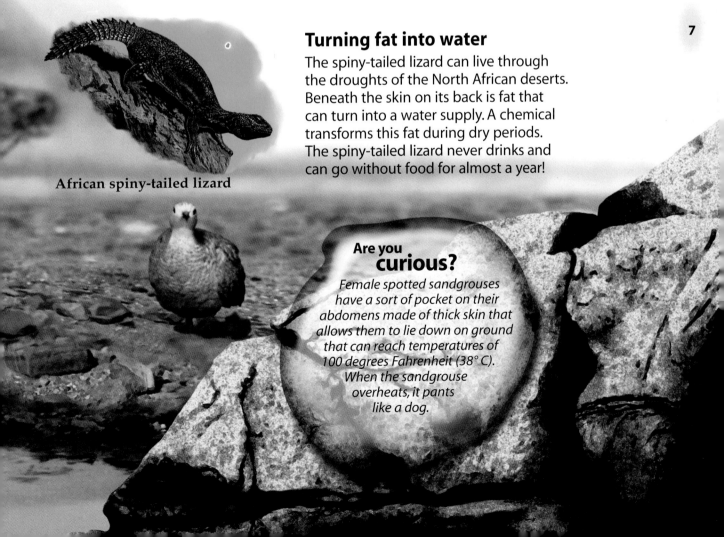

Are you curious?

Female spotted sandgrouses have a sort of pocket on their abdomens made of thick skin that allows them to lie down on ground that can reach temperatures of 100 degrees Fahrenheit (38° C). When the sandgrouse overheats, it pants like a dog.

Surviving the cold

Many animals do constant battle against the cold. There are places in the world where animals have had to adapt to fierce conditions. The Arctic Ocean, the frozen northern tundra, and the snow deserts of Antarctica — where the most powerful blizzards on the planet blow — are among the areas where only certain living beings can survive. For some of these animals, their survival actually depends on the existence of harsh climates.

Keeping warm

Nice and warm beneath its thick coat, the arctic fox, or white fox, is adapted to life in the frigid arctic climate. Long hair between its legs protect its skin from frostbite. Furthermore, very little heat leaves its body by way of its little round ears and short muzzle — extremities that are normally vulnerable to the cold.

8

arctic fox

An icebound seal

The Weddell seal is the mammal that lives closest to the South Pole in an environment of ice floes and icy-cold Antarctic waters. It can spend the polar winter in the water, beneath a thick layer of ice, because its dense fur and a layer of insulating fat keep it warm.

Weddell seal

Sugar-filled frogs

Hidden under a stone, the wood frog of North America has stopped breathing; its blood is no longer flowing through its veins; and most of the water in its body is frozen. This frog can survive being frozen for several weeks because it produces sugar that supplies energy to its organs and an antifreeze that keeps ice from forming inside its cells!

wood frog

9

A warm fur coat

A blizzard is raging on the vast arctic tundra. Huddled close together, about 20 musk oxen try to keep themselves warm. These mammals of the far north have a heavy fur coat that resists cold and moisture. Warmly wrapped up in this thick fleece, musk oxen can withstand extremely cold temperatures.

musk ox

Are you curious?

Like all mammals and birds, the fox has a control system that allows it to maintain a constant body temperature no matter what the outside temperature is. Animals such as invertebrates, fish, amphibians, and reptiles do not have this ability.

Fleeing winter

To flee or not to flee? Warmly muffled up in a thick layer of fat and wrapped in a heavy coat of fur, the best-equipped animals take on the cold. Others — insects, amphibians, and reptiles — surrender to it and freeze to death. Some take a long trip to warmer regions. Others — squirrels, hedgehogs, and bats — fall into a deep sleep until the warm days of spring arrive.

The big winter sleep

Cold weather, pale sunshine, and food shortages signal the beginning of winter. Rolled up in its burrow, the woodchuck, or groundhog, settles in to hibernate. It sleeps from mid-October to mid-March, feeding on the layer of fat it has built up in preparation for its long, restful winter.

woodchuck

Arctic travelers

The arctic cold never arrives alone. It is accompanied by food shortages. Without grasses, berries, seeds, or aquatic plants, the magnificent snow geese of North America leave the arctic tundra to seek refuge and food on the prairies of the southern United States and Mexico. In March, they head back north to reclaim the Arctic.

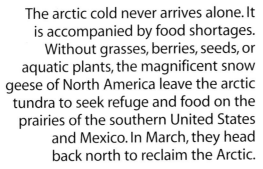

snow goose

A hibernating turtle

The small painted turtle was named for the colorful designs on its shell. This reptile lives in the ponds, lakes, and streams of the United States and Canada. It feeds on water plants, insect larvae, and small fish. In cold regions, it can spend up to 4 months hibernating in a burrow it digs in the mud.

painted turtle

A community refuge

In the fall, about 40 European adders curl up in the burrow of a rodent, in a crack in a rock, or under a tree trunk. They hibernate until spring comes. In some regions, they stay there for as long as 275 days! Rolled up and intertwined, the adders conserve their body heat.

adder

Are you curious?

During hibernation, the woodchuck lives in slow motion. Its body temperature drops, it breathes only about once every 5 minutes, and its heart beats just twice a minute. By the time it wakes up, it has lost about a third of its body weight!

The depths of the ocean

One of the darkest environments on Earth is 6,560 feet (2,000 m) and more beneath the surface of the ocean. No ray of sunshine penetrates these depths, and no green plant can live there. It was once believed that no animal could survive the blackness of this place. We now know that many animals live there — at depths of up to 36,000 feet (11,000 m) — in complete darkness, at very cold temperatures, and beneath the weight of a huge mass of water!

A vicious predator

The viperfish uses its long, fanglike teeth to skewer most of the few prey that venture near. This monster haunts temperate and tropical waters at depths of up to 8,200 feet (2,500 m). The jaw of the viperfish opens wide enough to make a mere mouthful of the shrimp and fish on which it lives!

12

viperfish

A deep-sea fisher

In the darkness of the ocean depths, animals must find their prey and defend themselves against enemies. Most of them create their own light. Some have spots of light on their bodies. Using the light bacteria on the top of its head, the deep-sea anglerfish lures prey toward its open mouth.

deep-sea anglerfish

deep-sea gulper eel

Where's the food?

In the depths of the ocean, food is scarce. The creatures that live there often have to make do with the plants and dead animals that drift down from above. The deep-sea gulper eel has a way to deal with this. One-quarter of its body is a huge head split by a giant mouth that can swallow a huge quantity of food at once.

The phantom of the depths

Giant squid really exist! However, no giant squid has ever been seen alive. The largest specimen found to date is 56 feet (17 m) long. In the darkness of the ocean depths, the enormous eyes of the giant squid probably allow the animal to spot its enemies as well as the prey it captures in its long tentacles.

giant squid

Are you curious?

The viperfish is a terrible swimmer. It allows itself to be carried by the current until one of its prey happens to drift near its mouth.

Raging waters

Life is often risky for aquatic animals. Whipped by waves or tossed about by tides, many animals cling desperately to life. Those that live in streams and rivers sometimes hurtle down mountains at dizzying speeds. The torrential waters offer little comfort to the animals that venture into them. Yet insects, crustaceans, mollusks, and fish grip stones or hide under them or conceal themselves inside a hard casing to hang on to life.

Walking on water

The dipper, or water ouzel, lives near fast-flowing streams. This bird finds its food under stones at the bottom of the water. With its tail spread wide, it clings to the streambed with its long claws and walks straight into the current. A skillful diver, it can also swim by tucking its feet against its body and using its wings as fins!

14

dipper

The stream stalker

The Szechwan (Tibetan) water shrew faces the swift waters of Asian streams with long webbed fingers, a tail that serves as a rudder, and a waterproof coat. The suckers on its feet help it cling to the slippery stones on the streambed and hold onto the prey it stalks at the bottom of the water.

Szechwan water shrew

Help from suckers

This tiny, flat-bodied fish has absolutely no fear of the strong currents in the streams of Southeast Asia! Acting somewhat like suckers, the large fins on the belly of the saddled hillstream loach enable it to cling to rocks at the bottom of the water, no matter how strong the current.

saddled hillstream loach

The water nymph

The stonefly larva can live in the icy, turbulent waters of streams and rivers. Its lungs allow it to breathe under the water. Its flat body does not disrupt the flow of the water and enables it to slide under stones. This larva also has claws that can cling to rocks and keep it from being carried away by the current.

stonefly larva

Are you curious?

Thanks to a thick layer of down and very dense plumage, the dipper can withstand extremely cold temperatures. Its skin glands secrete a large amount of fat that helps make its feathers waterproof.

On top of the mountains

The world's highest mountains are home to many forms of animal life. These living beings must brave cold temperatures, powerful winds, burning sunshine, and air without much oxygen. This situation would make it very difficult for many species to survive. However, some animals cope very well.

The giant of the mountains

This huge animal of Tibet sometimes ventures higher than 16,000 feet (5,000 m). Its long black hair protects it from violent winds, and its short undercoat of dense fur keeps its body warm. With its back to the wind and its head tucked against its front legs, the yak can withstand temperatures of -40 degrees Fahrenheit (-40°C)!

yak

The climbers' companion

This member of the crow family holds the bird record for survival at the highest altitude. Most birds would be unable to remain aloft in such thin air. The alpine chough's long wings help it execute skillful aerial maneuvers. This champion has been spotted at altitudes as high as 26,000 feet (8,000 m). It sometimes accompanies mountain climbers!

alpine chough

vicuña

Mammal of the high plateaus

At altitudes of 15,000 feet (4,500 m), human beings have trouble breathing and find the cold temperatures very painful. Wrapped in its wooly coat, however, the vicuña runs at speeds of over 28 miles (45 km) an hour! With large lungs and blood that carries lots of oxygen, this mammal enjoys its habitat.

alpine salamander

Safe eggs

Cold, wind, drought, and a lack of oxygen can be hard on the eggs of amphibians, reptiles, and insects. The alpine salamander keeps its eggs safe inside its body for as long as 4 years until they hatch! When the babies are finally born, they are ready to face life.

Are you curious?

Hemoglobin moves oxygen throughout the body. It carries more oxygen in animals that live at high altitudes than in those that live at sea level.

Deep in our planet

For millions of years, some amphibians, fish, and insects have been imprisoned in darkness, humidity, and cold in the depths of our planet. They have adapted to the cold temperatures, the darkness, and the lack of oxygen. American porcupines, bears, and certain bats and birds visit caves from time to time to rest or take refuge. Troglobites, however, live only in caves and could not survive outside their underground homes.

Blind fish

In the darkness of the deep, eyes are of no use. The blind cave tetras in the caves of Mexico are troglobites. These fish are born with eyes. But as they develop, their eyes sink into their heads until they are covered by a layer of skin. With no sight, they develop other senses, such as touch and smell.

blind cave tetra

olm

A cave-dwelling salamander

The olm is one of the strangest amphibians in the world. This little salamander lives in underground rivers and ponds. It has a pinkish, translucent body with three pairs of gills that allow the animal to breathe in the cold underground water. Like most cave-dwelling species, it is blind.

Cave echoes

Hundreds of oilbirds nest deep within North American mountain caves. To find their way around, they send their call over and over. The speed with which the echo returns tells them where obstacles are. This echo system enables the birds to fly through the caves without hurting themselves or getting lost!

oilbird

fungus gnat larva

A deadly light

Food is very scarce in underground streams. To find food, the larva of the fungus gnat has a clever trap. It hangs sticky threads from the top of a cave. This snare captures insects that are attracted by the pretty light produced by the body of the larva.

Are you curious?

Troglobites do not need skin pigments to protect them from the Sun. As a result, they are translucent. You can see the blood flowing through their pinkish flesh.

Pollution perils

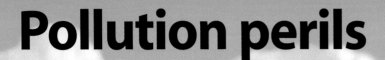

Pollution has put many animals in danger. Pesticides, herbicides, fertilizers, and metals such as mercury and lead have polluted Earth's ground, its groundwater, its lakes and rivers, its seas and oceans. The combustion of fuel pollutes the air and is raising the temperature of our planet. Rain brings the pollutants in the air to the ground and poisons the plants the animals eat.

Fragile shells

The pesticide DDT created a deadly chain reaction. Crustaceans whose flesh had been contaminated by DDT in seawater were eaten by fish. The fish in turn poisoned the pelicans that ate them. Female pelicans then began laying eggs with very thin shells. These fragile eggs cracked open before the chicks were ready to hatch.

brown pelican

A dwindling group

Only a few years ago, the beaches of the Mediterranean Sea were home to almost 5,000 monk seals. Today, only 700 seals live in the polluted waters of the sea. On the beaches, they have been replaced by sunbathers and motor vehicles. The polluted seawater is doing irreversible damage to the remaining monk seals.

Mediterranean monk seal

Mermaids in danger

dugong

The real-life inspiration for mermaids of legend, dugongs are among the world's most endangered animals. Once hunted for their flesh, their skin, and their fat, these giant sea mammals now must live in a dangerous habitat. The oil-polluted water of the Persian Gulf is severely damaging the dugong population.

Poisoned food

With a wingspan of up to 10 feet (3 m), the California condor is one of the largest birds in the world. It is also one of the most endangered. There are only about 120 of these birds left, most in captivity. Many were killed by hunters. Others were poisoned by swallowing the lead in the bodies of animals killed by hunters.

California condor

Are you curious?

In 1970, the brown pelican was placed on the list of endangered species. Since 1972, the use of DDT has been banned in the United States. Certain islands on which the pelicans nest have been turned into nature preserves. Though still in danger, the brown pelicans are doing better than before.

Endangered animals

A look at worldwide conditions shows an alarming picture. Forests are being destroyed each year. Coral reefs — enveloped by polluted water — have begun to die, endangering the animals that live there. Roads, housing developments, and shopping malls cover what once were fields and forests. Where will the animals go when driven from their homes?

Bad news, bears

In the wooded mountains of China, the giant panda feeds for 10 hours a day. Its favorite food is bamboo shoots, and it needs to eat 84 pounds (38 kilograms) daily! The few pandas that remain are facing a serious problem. The slopes once covered with bamboo have been cleared for farming and homes.

giant panda

Paradise in danger

The island of Madagascar was once a paradise in the Indian Ocean. Today, most of its forests have been cut down for farming. The indri, a large lemur, lives in the remaining forests and feeds on leaves and fruit. These primates cannot survive without the forests. Experts believe Madagascar's forests will be gone within just 30 years.

indri

babirusa

Pigs in peril

The wild pig called babirusa lives in the swamp forests of Indonesia. It may soon disappear forever. When disturbed, the females flee to the forest. They abandon their young, which have little chance of surviving on their own. The babirusa, hunted for meat, is losing its habitat to deforestation and mineral prospecting.

Declining amphibians

Amphibians lay their eggs on the edges of pools, ponds, lakes, and swamps. Deforestation and the filling in of wetlands have destroyed a huge number of their habitats. Because of this, amphibian populations are declining rapidly throughout the world.

Northern leopard frog

Are you curious?

At birth, the tiny panda weighs only 4.6 ounces (130 grams), or 900 times less than its mother! During the first 4 months of its life, it is carried by its mother, who takes it everywhere she goes. The baby panda cannot move around on its own until about the age of 5 months.

Extinct animals

Most of the species that have ever lived on our planet are now extinct; they no longer exist. This is a normal part of evolution. However, human beings have often speeded up this process. Among other actions, hunting and fishing; trading in the fur or skin of seals, big cats, and reptiles; and the selling of ivory have all contributed to the loss of certain species of animals.

A lost giant

The woolly mammoth, an ancestor of the modern elephant, lived about 10 million years ago on the tundra of Europe, Asia, and North America. These giants were hunted by prehistoric humans, who used its flesh for meat and its tusks as a building material for their houses.

woolly mammoth

Dead as a dodo

It took less than 200 years for settlers to wipe out the dodo birds of Mauritius. From the time it was discovered in 1598, this bird was hunted by human beings, pigs, dogs, and other animals. A bird that was said to be as dumb as a post, it built its nest on the ground. Because it could not fly away from its enemies, it is no longer with us.

dodo

The end of the dinosaurs

Human beings are not the only ones responsible for extinctions. No one knows exactly why the dinosaurs disappeared. An epidemic? A change in climate? A volcanic eruption? Today, we think that a meteor hit Earth about 65 million years ago. Triceratops — a huge, plant-eating dinosaur that lived about that time — is gone now.

triceratops

great auk

The last great auk

In 1830, an underwater volcanic eruption swallowed up the small islands on which the great auk — and hundreds of other kinds of birds — once nested. That disaster was not the only thing responsible for the loss of these large birds. Unable to fly, they were killed by human beings for their flesh and their fat. The last great auk was killed in 1844.

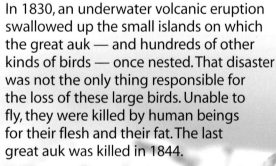

Are you curious?

Several frozen mammoths have been found in Alaska and Siberia. The color of their fur changed after death. In life, their coats were black. After death, because of a chemical reaction, their fur became a reddish color.

A map of where they live

1. **Brown-throated three-toed sloth (p. 2)**
   (South America)

2. **Hydrothermal vent tube worm (p. 3)**
   (Pacific Ocean)

3. **Peppered moth (p. 3)**
   (Europe, Asia)

4. **Lungfish (p. 3)**
   (Africa)

5. **Dromedary (p. 4)**
   (Africa, Middle East, Australia)

6. **Water-holding frog (p. 5)**
   (Australia)

7. **Namib Desert sand dune lizard (p. 5)**
   (Africa)

8. **Fennec (p. 5)**
   (Africa, Arabian peninsula)

9. **Spotted sandgrouse (p. 6)**
   (Africa, Asia)

10. **Desert darkling beetle (p. 7)**
    (Africa, the Middle East)

11. **Desert kangaroo rat (p. 7)**
    (southwestern United States)

12. **African spiny-tailed lizard (p. 7)**
    (Africa)

13. **Arctic fox (p. 8)**
    (North America, Europe, Asia)

14. **Weddell seal (p. 9)**
    (Antarctica)

15. **Musk ox (p. 9)**
    (Alaska, Canada, Greenland)

16. **Wood frog (p. 9)**
    (Alaska, Canada, United States)

17. **Woodchuck (p. 10)**
    (North America)

18. **Painted turtle (p. 11)**
    (Canada, United States)

19. **Snow goose (p. 11)**
    (North America, Greenland, Siberia, China, Japan, Mexico)

More fun facts

A HABITAT FOR EVERYONE	
Animal	**Extreme habitat**
Petroleum fly larvae	Oil pools
Brine shrimp	Salt marshes and salt lakes (the salt content of these environments is twice as high as that of the sea)
Salt creek pupfish	Volcanic lake containing no oxygen
Cyclopid copepod	
Pupfish	Water, 120 degrees Fahrenheit (49° C)
Mouthbrooder fish	Thermal springs
River trout	Cold, fast-running water
Black fly larvae	
Sea anemone	The world's oceans, from shorelines to the deepest trench
Limpet	Rocky coasts
African cave fish	Caves and caverns
Texas blind salamander	
Golden spider beetle	Potassium cyanide, cayenne pepper, ammonium chloride
Egyptian nightjar	Deserts, up to 140 degrees Fahrenheit (60° C)
Arctic hare	Polar regions
Emperor penguin	
Ringed seal	
Saddleback	
Jumping spider	Altitudes averaging 23,000 feet (7,000 m)
Luminous shrimp	Depths of the ocean, deeper than 16,400 feet (5,000 m)

ENDANGERED ANIMALS				
	Animal	**Geographic distribution**	**Population in nature**	**Main threats**
Insects	South American longhorn beetle	Brazil	Rare	Destruction of habitat, collectors
	Queen Alexandra's birdwing	New Guinea	Unknown	Destruction of habitat, collectors
Fish	Common Atlantic sturgeon	Portugal	Unknown	Overfishing, pollution
	Bluefin tuna	All oceans	Unknown	Overfishing, late sexual maturity (8 years)
	Gila trout	United States	Unknown	Pollution
Amphibians and reptiles	Golden toad	Costa Rica	May be extinct	Destruction of habitat
	American crocodile	United States, Mexico, South America, Central America, the Caribbean	About 200 to 300	Destruction of habitat, hunting
	Galapagos giant tortoise	Galapagos Islands	About 2,000	Predators, destruction of habitat
Birds	Mauritius kestrel	Mauritius	About 50	Destruction of habitat, predators, poisoning
	Siberian white crane	Siberia, China, Japan	About 1,400	Predators, trampling by herds of reindeer
	Crested ibis	Siberia, China, Japan	About 40	Destruction of habitat, pollution
	Dalmatian pelican	Europe, former Soviet Union	About 1,300 couples	Destruction of habitat, predators
Mammals	Black-footed ferret	Wyoming	About 130	Destruction of habitat, predators, poisoning, diseases
	Mountain gorilla	Africa	Fewer than 400	Destruction of habitat, poaching, diseases
	Arabian oryx	Arabia	About 100	Destruction of habitat
	Black rhinoceros	Africa	Fewer than 3,700	Destruction of habitat, poaching
	Tiger	Turkey, Europe, Asia	6,000 to 8,000	Hunting, destruction of habitat

29

For your information

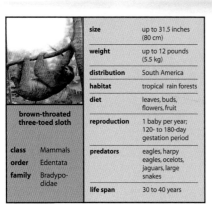

brown-throated three-toed sloth

size	up to 31.5 inches (80 cm)
weight	up to 12 pounds (5.5 kg)
distribution	South America
habitat	tropical rain forests
diet	leaves, buds, flowers, fruit
reproduction	1 baby per year; 120- to 180-day gestation period
predators	eagles, harpy eagles, ocelots, jaguars, large snakes
life span	30 to 40 years

class	Mammals
order	Edentata
family	Bradypo-didae

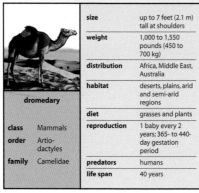

dromedary

size	up to 7 feet (2.1 m) tall at shoulders
weight	1,000 to 1,550 pounds (450 to 700 kg)
distribution	Africa, Middle East, Australia
habitat	deserts, plains, arid and semi-arid regions
diet	grasses and plants
reproduction	1 baby every 2 years; 365- to 440-day gestation period
predators	humans
life span	40 years

class	Mammals
order	Artio-dactyles
family	Camelidae

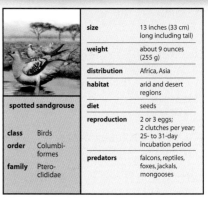

spotted sandgrouse

size	13 inches (33 cm) long including tail)
weight	about 9 ounces (255 g)
distribution	Africa, Asia
habitat	arid and desert regions
diet	seeds
reproduction	2 or 3 eggs; 2 clutches per year; 25- to 31-day incubation period
predators	falcons, reptiles, foxes, jackals, mongooses

class	Birds
order	Columbi-formes
family	Ptero-clididae

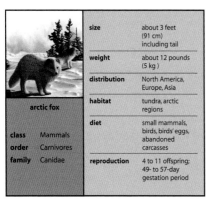

arctic fox

size	about 3 feet (91 cm) including tail
weight	about 12 pounds (5 kg)
distribution	North America, Europe, Asia
habitat	tundra, arctic regions
diet	small mammals, birds, birds' eggs, abandoned carcasses
reproduction	4 to 11 offspring; 49- to 57-day gestation period

class	Mammals
order	Carnivores
family	Canidae

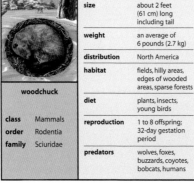

woodchuck

size	about 2 feet (61 cm) long including tail
weight	an average of 6 pounds (2.7 kg)
distribution	North America
habitat	fields, hilly areas, edges of wooded areas, sparse forests
diet	plants, insects, young birds
reproduction	1 to 8 offspring; 32-day gestation period
predators	wolves, foxes, buzzards, coyotes, bobcats, humans

class	Mammals
order	Rodentia
family	Sciuridae

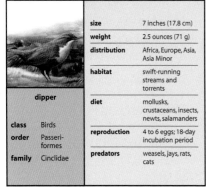

viperfish

size	about 8 inches (20 cm) long
distribution	Atlantic, Pacific, and Indian Oceans; Mediterranean Sea
habitat	deep water; depths of up to 8,200 feet (2,500 m)
diet	crustaceans, fish

class	Fish
order	Stomiiformes
family	Chaulio-dontidae

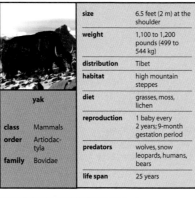

dipper

size	7 inches (17.8 cm)
weight	2.5 ounces (71 g)
distribution	Africa, Europe, Asia, Asia Minor
habitat	swift-running streams and torrents
diet	mollusks, crustaceans, insects, newts, salamanders
reproduction	4 to 6 eggs; 18-day incubation period
predators	weasels, jays, rats, cats

class	Birds
order	Passeri-formes
family	Cinclidae

yak

size	6.5 feet (2 m) at the shoulder
weight	1,100 to 1,200 pounds (499 to 544 kg)
distribution	Tibet
habitat	high mountain steppes
diet	grasses, moss, lichen
reproduction	1 baby every 2 years; 9-month gestation period
predators	wolves, snow leopards, humans, bears
life span	25 years

class	Mammals
order	Artiodac-tyla
family	Bovidae

blind cave tetra

size	3 inches (7.6 cm)
distribution	United States, Mexico
habitat	underground rivers
diet	invertebrates, fish, aquatic plants

class	Fish
order	Cyprini-formes
family	Characidae

brown pelican

size	3 to 4.5 feet (1 to 1.4 m) long
weight	7 to 8 pounds (3.2 to 3.6 kg)
distribution	United States, South America, West Indies, Galapagos Islands
habitat	bays, estuaries, and lagoons
diet	fish, shrimp
reproduction	2 to 3 eggs; 30-day incubation period

class	Birds
order	Pelecani-formes
family	Pelecanidae

giant panda

size	4 to 5 feet (1.2 to 1.5 m) long
distribution	China
habitat	mountains on which bamboo grows
diet	bamboo
reproduction	1 baby; 97- to 163-day gestation period
life span	at least 15 years

class	Mammals
order	Carnivora
family	Procyo-nidae

woolly mammoth

size	14 feet (4.2 m) tall at the shoulders; tusks up to 13 feet (4 m) long
distribution	Europe, Siberia, North America
habitat	tundra and cold regions
diet	grasses and leaves
predators	humans

class	Mammals
order	Probos-cidea
family	Proboscidea

Glossary

amphibian: An animal that can live on land or in water

Antarctica: A geographical area around the South Pole

aquatic: Growing or living in water

Arctic: A geographical area around the North Pole

blizzard: A strong winter wind accompanied by heavy snow

camouflage: A disguise meant to hide an animal from its enemies

combustion: An act of burning

crustacean: Any of a class of animals that have shells and many pairs of legs

deforestation: Excessive tree clearing that destroys a forest

dehydration: The process of losing body fluids, such as water, and drying out

den: A hollow or cave that serves as a refuge or shelter for a wild animal

drought: A prolonged shortage of water

fertilizer: A substance used on soil to make it more fertile

frostbite: The destruction of tissues by freezing, mainly in the nose, fingers, and toes

gestation: The period during which a female human or animal carries her offspring before birth

gill: An organ of an animal such as a fish that allows it to breathe

gland: An organ that produces a secretion

habitat: The environment where a plant or an animal lives

herbicide: A substance used to control weeds

hibernate: To spend the winter in a resting state

hostile: Not hospitable, as an environment that makes life very difficult

ice floe: In polar regions, a huge mass of floating ice

invertebrate: An animal without a spine

irreversible: Not able to be reversed or returned to a former state

larva: An often wormlike form that is one stage of an animal's life

mineral prospecting: An exploration of an area conducted to locate mineral deposits

mollusk: An animal with a soft body that has no bones but usually has a hard shell

offspring: All of the children or young of a human or animal

pesticide: A substance used to kill pests of any kind that attack crops

pollution: The dirtying or poisoning of Earth's air, soil, or water

predator: An animal that destroys or eats another

prey: An animal that is the victim of a predator

primate: An order of mammals that includes human beings, apes, monkeys, and some related animals

reptile: A crawling animal with scale-covered skin, such as the snake, the iguana, and the tortoise

secrete: To form and give off from the body

temperate: Moderate, referring to a climate that does not have extreme temperatures

tentacle: An elongated, flexible arm, often lined with suckers, used by certain mollusks to touch and grasp

translucent: Allowing light to pass through but not transparent enough to allow objects to be seen clearly

tropical: Relating to or occurring in a frost-free climate with warm temperatures

tundra: A cold region where the vegetation is limited to moss, lichen, and a few other plants

vent: A vertical channel or conduit that allows substances to rise up and emerge from Earth's surface

water: To provide with drinking water

Index

Editorial Director Caroline Fortin **Research and Documentation** Anne-Marie Brault, Kathleen Wynd **Page Setup** Chantal Boyer **Illustrations** Jocelyn Gardner
Translator Gordon Martin **Copy Editing** Veronica Schami **Gareth Stevens editing** Joan Downing **Cover Design** Joel Bucaro, Scott Krall

19544031R00061

Made in the USA
Lexington, KY
28 November 2018